M000033566

The Official Rules
for
Golfers

**Other Official Rules Books
by Paul Dickson
Published by Walker and Company**

*The Official Rules at Home
The Official Rules at Work
The Official Rules for Lawyers, Politicians
. . . and Everyone They Torment*

The Official Rules
for
Golfers

Paul Dickson

Walker and Company
New York

Copyright © 1997 by Paul Dickson
Illustrations copyright © 1997 by Steven Guarnaccia

All rights reserved. No part of this book may be reproduced
or transmitted in any form or by any means, electronic or
mechanical, including photocopying, recording, or by any
information storage and retrieval system, without permis-
sion in writing from the Publisher.

First published in the United States of America in 1997 by
Walker Publishing Company, Inc.

Published simultaneously in Canada by Thomas Allen &
Son Canada, Limited, Markham, Ontario

Library of Congress Cataloging-in-Publication Data
Dickson, Paul.
      The official rules for golfers/Paul Dickson.
           p. cm.
      Includes index.
      ISBN 0-8027-1327-0
      1. Golf—Quotations, maxims, etc. 2. Golf—Rules—
Humor.
   I. Title.
   GV967.D54 1997
   796.352'02'07—dc21   97-7816
                                                  CIP

Book design by James McGuire

Printed in the United States of America

10 9 8 7 6 5 4 3 2 1

Dedicated to my late father,
William A. Dickson, Jr., who loved golf for
all the right reasons.

The Official Rules
for
Golfers

CALAMITAS NECESSARIA EST

Introduction

Golfers possess a remarkable view of the cosmos.
  We blame fate for most accidents but feel personally responsible for a hole in one.
  We understand that a round of golf adds up to 100 strokes more or less (if we should ever be so lucky) and realize that this gives 100 chances, more or less, to go awry.
  Awry is a technical golfing term for the fact that there are an infinite number of mistakes that can be made on any given shot. As one student of the inept once pointed out, even swinging at and completely missing the ball can be achieved "in different ways for different reasons."
  For us golf is a friendly but powerful obsession that invades all our waking thoughts and leaves us with few diversions that don't remind us of the game. I know I'm not the only one who saw *Jurassic Park* and scoffed at the whole preposterous premise of the movie: i.e., that a resort could be created, charge guests $10,000 a day, and *not* offer golf.
  We are painfully aware that we play a game

with a ball that is 1½ inches in diameter and all too often end up hitting the ball it rests on, which is 8,000 miles in diameter.

We *know* that the game promises one part glory to ninety-nine parts humility. As Alistair Cooke put it, "Golf is an open exhibition of overweening ambition, courage deflated by stupidity, skill soured by a whiff of arrogance," adding, "These humiliations are the essence of the game."

Yet we keep plugging away at it. What it all points to is the inescapable conclusion that golf is a grand paradigm that, when reduced to a simple equation, reads like this:

$$LI = G + \text{or} -$$

Life Itself (LI) equals Golf (G) more (+) or less (-). Few have come to this conclusion as eloquently as W. Hastings Webling, who introduced his 1909 collection of golf verse, *Fore! The Call of the Links*, with these lines: "The game is like life because it develops so many lost opportunities, and certainly life is the source of all humor. Again it is like life because it brings moments of ecstatic happiness. It produces inspiration, and inspiration begets poetry."

Once this is understood, it becomes clear that most of the more pointed things that have been said about golf are on par with more universal truths. "Never give up," said Tom Watson of golf. "If we give up in this game, we'll give up on life."

Jim Murray of the Los Angeles *Times* sees it as the darker side of life: "Golf is the cruelest of sports. Like life, it's unfair. It's a harlot! A trollop. It leads you on. It never lives up to its promises. It's not a sport, it's bondage. An obsession. A boulevard of broken dreams."

Of course, not everyone would agree. "Golf is neither a microcosm of nor a metaphor for Life," wrote Dick Schaap in *Massacre at Winged Foot*. "It is a sport, a bloodless sport, if you don't count ulcers." Schaap is of course wrong on several counts, not the least of which is the fact that meetings and telephones, not golf, cause ulcers.

Because golf and life mimic each other and vice versa, golfers have long sought comfort in words: aphorisms, blessings, curses, tips, and so on. We are also on a constant quest for the Rosetta Stone of the game, a set of infallible rules and admonitions that would make us better golfers. Trouble is, most rules and admonitions are aimed at making us better human beings not straightening out an iron shot. The quest is constant.

Which brings us to the role of the Murphy Center for the Codification of Human and Organizational Law and the collection of rules that follows.

Readers of previous Official Rules books know that the Murphy Center was founded in 1976 by the compiler of this collection, who was its first

Director, and has been, since 1989, its self-appointed Director for Life. It was inspired by and named for Murphy's Law ("If anything can go wrong, it will"), and it set out to codify the truths and realities of work, home, and play in these imperfect times. It is housed in a growing pile of shoe boxes (this topical collection is, in fact, housed in a golf shoe box that has been dubbed the Murphy Center Golf Club, the first and only official adjunct facility to the Murphy Center).

Why did this august body veer off course to study golf?

The answer is simple: The Murphy Center has long been interested in the study of such quirky phenomena as the often perverse behavior of inanimate objects, aberrant human behavior, and various cosmic ironies. What better laboratory for studying these things than the golf course? We will continue our quest for understanding, and the readers of this small, scientific work are encouraged to send the results of their research to the Center/Club (P.O. Box 80, Garrett Park, MD 20896).

One problem that begs to be worked on is that of bodies of magnetized water which dot the landscape. A case in point: During the summer of 1996, a local public course installed a formidable lake as a hazard for both the 7th and 8th holes that at first glance appeared to be about forty fathoms deep and a quarter mile across. On my very first attempt to play over and around this inland sea, in October 1996, I lost no fewer than (but maybe more than) five balls, each sailing like a perfect curveball right smack into the drink.

Was the lake telling me of its sovereignty? Were sunspots to blame? Was my son Alex, with whom I was playing, to blame for babbling on about keeping my eye on the ball rather than looking transfixed at the damned ocean? Is some top-secret CIA/military project involved? I need help with this problem, because all I know for sure is that it was not my fault.

The items that follow were collected over a period of years and are listed alphabetically by the name of the law, effect, or principle. There will be some rules attributed to Anon. and Trad., which usually are short for anonymous and traditional—the Murphy Center, however, thinks of them as hapless golfing buddies named Anon. and Trad.

In addition to the main body of the book, the readers are offered a series of special sections ("Don'ts for the Duffer," "Fables for Golfers," "How to Make a Hole in One," "Pillow Talk," "Revised Proverbs," "The 'Rules of Golf' Revised," "Shakespeare the Golfer," "Signs, Rules, and Committee Postings Reportedly Found on

Clubhouse Bulletin Boards and in Pro Shops Worldwide," "Tee Talk," and "Wodehouse's Three Best Golfing Lines") and two bonus sections at the back of the book (a collection called "Toasts, Jokes, Etc.—Equipment for the 19th Hole" and a "Glossary of Important Golfing Terms").

Fore!

A

•**Aaron's Calculation.** It took me seventeen years to get 3,000 hits in baseball. I did it in one afternoon on the golf course.

> —Baseball Hall of Famer
> Hank Aaron

•**Adams's Admonition.** If you break 100, watch your golf. If you break 80, watch your business.

> —Comic Joey Adams

•**Advice to Duffer Putters.** Keep it low!

> —Bob Sterling, quoted by Bennett Cerf in his book *Life of the Party* (1956). The comment was made after a duffer asked Sterling for advice on making a ten-foot putt that would bring him in under 125 for the first time in his life.

•**Agnes Allen's Law.** Almost anything is easier to get into than out of.

> —Agnes Allen, whose law was written for a host of situations (marriage, jail, contracts, etc.) but is particularly appropriate to golf. She was the wife of famous historian Frederick Lewis Allen, who wrote of her law: "At one stroke human wisdom had been advanced to an unprecedented degree."

•**Anon.'s Law of the Tee.** Golf matches are not won on the fairways or greens. They are won on the tee—the first tee.

> —Anon., quoted in Bobby Riggs's *Court Hustler* (1973)

•**Anon.'s Delineation.** The mark of a champion is the ability to make the most of good luck and the best of bad.

> —Anon., quoted in George Houghton's book *Believe It or Not That's Golf* (1974)

•**Anon.'s Lesson of Links.** There is no mystery about golf, on every tee there is a marker telling you how many strokes to take to the next hole.

> —Quoted in Robert Cromie's *Par for the Course* (1964)

•**Anson's Putting Proposition.** I would rather face the best pitcher that ever lived than be called upon to make a three-foot putt at a critical point of a golf match.

> —A. C. "Cap" Anson, famous baseball player, who was the greatest hitter of his day

•**Archer's Admission.** If it wasn't for golf, I'd probably be a caddie today.

> —Pro golfer George Archer, in *Sports Illustrated*, July 28, 1980

•Armour's Conclusion. There's no need to tell one who has played a great deal of championship golf that it's the short game that decides the contests.

> —Golf pro Tommy Armour (1895–1968), in his book *How to Play Your Best Golf All the Time* (1953)

•Lord Avebury's Summation on Golf and Life.
Keep your eye on the ball.
Keep straight.
Keep in the course.
Take time.
Do not press.
Not up, not in.
Do not lose heart.
Be temperate in all things, and
Keep your temper or you will lose your game.

> —Lord Avebury, quoted in *The Pro and Con of Golf* by Alexander H. Revell (1915)

•Axiom of the Stick. What matters is not the length of the wand, but the magic in the stick.

> —Anon.

B

•**Lord Bacon's Advice to Those Who Would Laugh at an Opponent.** *In calamitoso, risus etiam injuria*—In misfortune, even to smile is to offend.

>—Lord Bacon, quoted in *The Pro and Con of Golf* by Alexander H. Revell (1915)

•**Baker's Advice.** Golf should never be talked about in a sitting position. The lecturer, in order to gain maximum effectiveness, should act out his stories.

>—Stephen Baker, 1962

•**Bantock's Revision.**
I drove a ball into the air,
It fell to earth, I know not where;
But if I'd found it, I'll bet you,
I would have done that hole in two!

>—Miles Bantock, from his 1901 work *On Many Greens*

•**Barber's Admission.** I don't say my golf game is bad, but if I grew tomatoes, they'd come up sliced.

—Golfer Miller Barber

•**Barnicle's Comparison.** Golf is the equivalent of crack for middle-aged white men.

—Mike Barnicle in his *Boston Globe* column, July 15, 1990

•**Batchelor's Proverbs.** (1) It is an unwise pro that beats his only pupil. (2) The longer the grass, the shorter the temper. (3) Putt in haste and repent at leisure. (4) Up all night, down all day. (5) The hole is greater than a half.

—Gerald Batchelor, quoted in *In Praise of Golf* by Webster Evans and Tom Scott (1950)

•**Bo Diddley's Advice to Golfers.** Don't let your mouth write no check that your tail can't cash.

—Bo Diddley

•**Boros Beatitude.** Swing easy, hit hard.

—Golf pro Julius Boros

•**Broun's Distinction.** Golf is not, on the whole, a game for realists. By its exactitudes of measurement it invites the attention of perfectionists.

> —Heywood Hale Broun, in
> his 1979 *Tumultuous*
> *Merriment*

C

•**Campbell's Economic Truism.** Trade follows the golf stick.

> —Patrick Campbell in his 1963 work *How to Become a Scratch Golfer.* In the book a fictional British captain of industry is telling his son why he will work for his company and play golf.

•**Cannon's Razor.** People who wear white shoes are either golfers or tourists.

> —Author Jimmy Cannon, quoted in Al Carrell and Don January's book *Golf Is a Funny Game* (1967)

•**Carter's Bowling Truism.** One of the advantages bowling has over golf is that you very seldom lose a bowling ball.

> —Don Carter, bowling great

•**Carver's Hint.** Anything will give up its secrets if you love it enough.

> —George Washington Carver

•**Carey's First Commandment.** THOU
SHALT NOT REPLACE ANY DIVOT OVER SIX
INCHES (any divot that big will no longer be
considered a divot but will officially be deemed
"sod." Lift it, take it home, and plant it in your
backyard).

> —Tom Carey, Chicago, from
> *Teed Off*

•**Casper's Secret.** Golf should be played, not
practiced.

> —Billy Casper, asked for the
> secret of his success at the
> game, and quoted in David
> Guiney, *The Dunlop Book of
> Golf* (1973)

•**Chi Chi's Conclusions.** (1) It's when they
call you lucky that you know you're good. (2)
Golf is the most fun you can have with your
clothes on.

> —Golfer Chi Chi Rodriguez,
> 1990. He is also a disputer of
> axioms. Keep your eye on
> the ball? "The USGA has a
> machine that can hit a golf
> ball three hundred yards
> every time," says Chi Chi,
> "and it's never seen a golf
> ball."

•Crenshaw's Admonition. Never do anything stupid.

> —Golfer Ben Crenshaw, who also gives us:

•Crenshaw's Test on Determining if You Are in a Rut. A couple of weeks ago I went fishing, and on the first cast I missed the lake.

•Cunningham's Definition. A game in which a ball 1½ inches in diameter is placed on a ball 8,000 miles in diameter. The object is to hit the small ball but not the large.

> —John Cunningham

D

•**Daly's Dilemma.** Golf is like a love affair: if you don't take it seriously, it's no fun; if you do take it seriously, it breaks your heart.

> —Sportswriter Arnold Daly
> (1904–74), quoted in *Reader's Digest*, November 1933

•**Darwin's Disclaimer.** Golf is not a funeral, though both can be very sad affairs.

> —Bernard Darwin
> (1876–1961), who is also the author of:

•**Darwin's Law.** It is a law of nature that everybody plays a hole badly when playing through.

> —The irony of this law by Bernard Darwin is that he was the grandson of the famous naturalist Charles Darwin, author of the other Darwin's Law—the one having to do with natural selection. One of the great golf

writers of all time, Darwin was a well-established lawyer who threw it all away in 1907 for half a century of great golf writing.

•**Demaret's Conclusion.** You can always recover from a bad drive, but there's no recovering from a bad putt. It's missing those six-inchers that causes us to break up our sticks.

> —Pro Jimmy Demaret (1910–1984), quoted in the *Saturday Evening Post*

•**DeVicenzo's Comparison.** Golf is like love. One day you think you're too old, and the next you can't wait to do it again.

> —Roberto DeVicenzo, quoted by columnist Hubert Mizell in the *St. Petersburg Times* February 21, 1990

•**Dickson's Determination.** Practice does not make perfect. Practice often compounds errors. Golf, sex, and child rearing prove this.

> —Paul Dickson, compiler of this book

•**Diller's Discovery.** The reason the pro tells you to keep your head down is so you can't see him laughing.

> —Phyllis Diller, quoted in
> Carol Mann's *The 19th Hole*
> (1992)

Don'ts for the Duffer

Golf is a game of do's and don'ts. The Murphy Center offers some of the latter:

•Don't read the rules; they interfere with your judgment.
•Don't be obsessed with the etiquette of the

game if you are a beginner. Trial and error is a time-tested method for learning proper behavior.

•Don't improve your lie while your opponent is looking.

•Don't ask a two-handicap man to play with you, and expect him to be pleased with your game.

•Don't count a "swing over"; it is not fair to your score.

•Don't play a bad lie; it might injure your club.

•Don't talk for more than five minutes on the putting green after you have holed out; it delays your game.

•Don't ever give up on a lost ball. If a lost ball is not found within twenty to twenty-five minutes, it is a good idea to signal the group behind you to come up and assist.

•Don't hesitate to stop and take a full swing at every dandelion, goose dropping, and cigar butt in your path. It will sharpen your skills.

•Don't fail to blame the greens committee for your bad shots.

•Don't neglect to hustle those ahead; any delay is an injustice to those following you.

•Don't call your golf sticks such an ordinary name as clubs; "bats" is much snappier.

•Don't hesitate to play the ball with the better lie; give the other person a worthy challenge.

•Don't extinguish lit cigarettes and cigars in the

sand traps—they are *not* ashtrays. Rather, leave your lit butts on the green as a greeting to the next foursome. They will thank you, since the acrid smoke from the burning grass and tobacco acts to discourage insects.

•Don't miss the opportunity to linger on the green and practice your putting.

•Don't worry about damage to the course: Part of your greens fee goes to greenkeepers who are paid good money to worry about such things.

•Don't forget, golf is combat. Politeness, charm, wit, and sympathy are encumbrances. When money is at stake, jangle the coins in your pocket when your opponent is putting.

> —The original list of these "Don'ts" appears in *The Pro and Con of Golf* by Alexander H. Revell (1915) and are attributed to "Niblicking," presumably the author's evil golf alter ego. Others have been added by the Director.

•**Dooley's Definition.** A game you play with your worst enemy—yourself.

> —American humorist Finley Peter Dunne (1867–1936), in the guise of his comic figure

"Mr. Dooley." The full quote
in the original written dialect
of Dooley: "In a gin'ral way,
all I can say about it is that
it's a kind iv game that ye
play with ye'er own worst
inimy, which is ye'ersilf."

•**Duffer's Laws.** (1) No matter how bad a
round of golf you play, there will always be at
least one stroke so perfect, so on target, and so
gratifying that you will come back to play again.
(2) The best way for a Duffer to go around a
tree standing directly in his line is to aim directly at the tree, since you never hit where you aim
anyway. (3) The only time you'll ever hit the
ball straight is when you're applying Duffer's
Law #2. (4) Never carry more clubs than you
can afford to break. (5) It is a myth that playing
an old ball guarantees you will carry the lake.
(6) Nobody cares what you shot today except
you.

—In 1980, the author of this
article published a book of
revealed wisdom (revealed to
others, collected by me)
called *The Official
Explanations.* It carried a set
of laws penned in pain by a
man who was then a star

writer for *Washingtonian*, John H. Corcoran, Jr., who first wrote down these rules on a 19th hole cocktail napkin. This body of laws was revolutionary in that it was the first attempt to take golf and reduce it to law, a crude thermodynamics of the game, if you will.

The first of these laws may be, in the estimation of this observer, the most important and compelling ever set down on napkin.

E

•**Eisenhower's Lament.** A lot more people beat me now.

> —President Dwight David Eisenhower (1890–1969), after leaving the White House in 1960. This may be a constant for former chief executives who golf: In 1994, former president George Bush was asked how his life had changed since he left the White House: "Well, for one thing, I find that I no longer win every golf game I play."

•**Emerson's Omission.** Nature never hurries: Atom by atom, little by little, she achieves her work. The lesson one learns in fishing, yachting, hunting, or planting is the manners of Nature: patience with many delays.

> —Ralph Waldo Emerson, who left golf off the list presumably because he did not wish to do anything to popu-

larize the game and make it
harder to get a tee time for
himself

•**Essex Golf Club Analogy.** Golf is a form of
work made expensive enough for rich men to
enjoy. It is physical and mental exertion made
attractive by the fact that you have to dress for
it in a $200,000 clubhouse. Golf is what letter
carrying, ditch digging, and carpet beating
would be if those tasks could be performed on
the same hot afternoon in short pants and col-
ored socks by gouty-looking gentlemen who
require a different implement for each mood.
Golf is the simplest-looking game in the world
when you decide to take it up and the toughest-
looking after you have been at it ten or twelve
years. It is probably the only known game a
man can play as long as a quarter of a century,
and then discover that it was too deep for him
in the first place.

—These comments have been
circulating for many years
with the attribution "Essex
Golf and Country Club News"
or simply written on a sheet
of paper with the question
"What is this golf?" and
attributed to "Author
Unknown." One Anon. ver-

sion in a 1966 issue of *Golf Digest* contained several other points, including this one: "Golf is played on carefully selected grass with little white balls and as many clubs as the player can afford. These balls usually cost from 50 cents to $2.00, and it is possible to support a family for months on the money represented by the balls lost by some golfers in a single afternoon."

F

Fables for Golfers

The Fable of the Crow

A golfer sliced his tee shot into the woods, where it landed in a crow's nest. When Papa Crow came home, he mistook the golf ball for an egg, and was so elated that he refused even to listen to Mama Crow's explanation. For years he had waited for offspring, and now success seemed imminent.

He ordered Mama Crow to begin hatching at once. She tried to reason with him, but in vain. He was obsessed with the idea of a baby crow.

Reluctantly, Mama Crow took her position over the golf ball egg. She sat on it for a whole month, twisting and turning. All the while, Papa Crow watched with keen anticipation.

When it became obvious that the egg would not hatch, Papa Crow became furious. He accused his mate of incompetence and ordered her from the nest. Sadly, she took her leave, never to return.

What Papa Crow never realized, but Mama

Crow knew all along, was that you never can get a birdie by topping a golf ball.
> —From *How to Break 90 Before You Reach It* by Sidney "Steve" Brody (1967)

The Fable of the Lost Motorist

A motorist is lost on the back roads of rural Georgia. He stops to ask for directions at a ramshackle wooden structure with a fading sign that promises Eat-Gas-Live Bait.

"Beg pardon," the motorist says to an old gent in grease-stained overalls. "Can you tell me how to get to the Masters in Augusta?" The old gent squints, grunts, and lets fly a stream of tobacco juice. Finally he wipes his stubby beard with the back of his hand and drawls: "Practice, practice, practice."

> —Variation on old theme. This version from Glen Waggoner's *Divots, Shanks, Gimmies, Mulligans and Chili Dips.*

•**Fitch's Principles of Golfing.** (1) Golf, to the timid man who has mowed a large field with a dull club for the first time, is an overgrown game of hide-and-seek which is played on a reformed cow pasture with clubs and a vocabu-

lary. (2) **A** golf course consists of eighteen four-
and-a-half-inch holes of the best quality, carefully concealed about a one-hundred-and-eighty-
acre field. The object of the game is to put an
undersized rubber ball into each of the holes in
succession without breaking a blood-vessel.
(3) The clubs which are used in herding the ball
over the course are many in number. (4) The
rules of the game are very simple. You must hit
the ball with your club. After you have hit it
you must find it, of course, before you hit it
again. It will take you several weeks to master
these two rules. After driving the ball you must
hit it wherever it lies. Good lies are as important in golf as in fishing. Losing a ball costs you
two strokes and fifty cents.

> —George Fitch, who articu-
> lated this in his 1909 master-
> piece *Golf for the Beginner,*
> when, it seems, golf balls cost
> about the same as a decent
> lunch at the club

•Fitzgerald's Truth. A golf course is nothing
but a poolroom moved outdoors.

> —Barry Fitzgerald, declining
> an invitation to hit the links
> with Bing Crosby in the
> movie *Going My Way*

•Forbes's Razor. Golf is an ideal diversion, but a ruinous disease.

—B. C. Forbes, *Epigrams*

•Ford's Conclusion. I have never seen a [golf] tournament, regardless of how much money or fame or prestige or emotion was involved, that didn't end with the victor extending his hand to the vanquished. The pat on the back, the arm around the shoulder, the praise for what was done right and the sympathetic nod for what wasn't are as much a part of golf as life itself. I would hope that understanding and reconciliation are not limited to the 19th hole alone.

—Gerald R. Ford, at the dedication of the World Golf Hall of Fame, Pinehurst, North Carolina, September 11, 1974

•Funston's Rule. Always expect your opponent to hole out on his next stroke and you will never be surprised.

—Attributed to Irv Funston, a Michigan Seniors champion

G

•Gallico's Razor. If there is any larceny in a man, golf will bring it out.

> —Novelist Paul Gallico (1897–1976), quoted in the *New York Times,* March 6, 1977

•Gobel's Geographical Observation. Where I play, the greens always break toward the bar.

> —Comedian and early television star "Lonesome" George Gobel (1920–1991), responding to another golfer quoting

Ben Hogan's observation that greens near the ocean break imperceptibly toward the sea. Gobel's response was recorded in Fred Beck's 1956 *To Hell With Golf*.

•**Golf's Distinction.** Golf is the only sport in which the participants routinely talk to the ball.
—Anon. The *Boston Globe* reported President Bill Clinton's immortal words to his ball after teeing off on a Martha's Vineyard golf course in August 1993: "Whoa! Momma, stay up."

•**Graffis's Estimate, or Why Are There So Many Breaches of Golf Etiquette?** It has been estimated that a golfer's chances of making a hole in one are much greater than the probability that he will read the rules of the game.
—Herb Graffis, *Esquire's World of Golf* (1933)

•**Graham's Short History of Golf.** Golf was invented by some Scotsman who hit a ball, with a stick, into a hole in the ground. The game today is exactly the same, except that it now takes some ninety-odd pages of small type to ensure that the ball is hit with the stick into the hole in the ground *without cheating.*

> —British writer A. S. Graham, in his book *Graham's Golf Club* (1965)

•Graham's Theological Exception. Prayer never seems to work for me on the golf course. I think this has something to do with my being a terrible putter.

> —The Reverend Billy Graham, quoted in *Golf's Most Outrageous Quotes: An Official Bad Golfers Association Book* by Bruce Nash and Allan Zullo with Bill Hartigan

•Gross's Golfing Confession. I've lost balls in every hazard and on every course I've tried, but when I lose a ball in the ball washer it's time to take stock.

> —Milton Gross, in his classic
> *Eighteen Holes in My Head*
> (1959)

•Gulbenkian's Razor. I find it more satisfying to be a bad player at golf. The worse you play, the better you remember the occasional good shot.

> —Nubar Gulbenkian, quoted
> in his *London Daily Telegraph*
> obituary, January 12, 1972

H

•**Hagen's Explanation.** I was dead scared I might finish 56th.

> —Walter Hagen (1892–1969), asked why he was playing so hard in the second round of the 1920 British Open after a poor first round. He finished in 55th place.

•**Hanley's Observation.** By itself, practice does not make perfect. Those of us with a ten-year-old son practicing the trumpet may understand that.

> —Dr. Daniel Hanley

•**Herold's Truth.** You can't alibi a 100 score down to 80.

> —Humorist and cartoonist Don Herold, in *Love That Golf* (1951)

•**Hogan's Distinction.** There is no similarity between golf and putting; they are two different

games. One is played in the air and the other on the ground.
>—Ben Hogan, quoted in *A Passion for the Game of Golf*

•**Hogan's Dream.** I once had a dream where I made seventeen straight holes in one and I lipped out my tee shot on the 18th hole. I was so goddamned mad I couldn't sleep.
>—Ben Hogan, quoted in *Sports Illustrated*, June 20, 1988

•**Hope's Best Line About Former President Gerald Ford.** His wife formed the Betty Ford Clinic—it can cure anything but Jerry's slice.
>—Bob Hope, quoted in *USA Today*, March 30, 1987

•**Hope's Distinction.** If you watch a game, it's fun. If you play, it's recreation. If you work at it, it's golf.
>—Bob Hope, quoted in *Reader's Digest*, October 1958

•**Hope's Exit Line.** I have to go now. I'm a little short of cash and I just saw a guy with wooden shafts get off the Denver bus.
>—Bob Hope, in Vic Fredericks's *For Golfers Only*

(1964). Hope dropped the
line to end an informal TV
interview done right on a golf
course.

•**Hornsby's Distinction.**   When I hit a ball, I
want somebody else to go chase it.
>   —Rogers Hornsby, baseball
>   great

How to Make a Hole in One

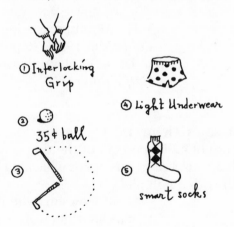

No book with the term "golf" or "golfer" in its
title is worth its price without some practical
stroke-saving advice. Here, then, is the obligato-

ry and long-awaited Club Murphy single best
piece of "how to" information.

In making a hole in one I stand with the feet
fairly wide apart and the weight evenly distrib-
uted on both heels. I use the interlocking grip,
a three-quarters swing, a thirty-five-cent ball,
and the regulation prayer.

I generally wear light underwear, as there is
nothing that will upset a stroke more than the
itch that comes from a woolen or hair-lined
undershirt at the moment of the upswing, and
prefer golf socks that are smart without being
vulgar.

> —H. I. Phillips, writing in
> *Collier's* in 1930. Republished
> in Dave Stanley's *Treasury of
> Golf Humor*

•**Howson's Theorem.** On the average, a
maximum of 4.097 percent of the time associated with a round of golf is spent whacking the
golf ball with a golf club.

> —Geoff Howson, who proves
> this in his 1988 work *Golf:
> How to Look Good When
> You're Not* (Contemporary
> Books), which is devoted to
> mastering the many non-golf-

ball-striking activities associated with the game, such as walking, talking, and harassing the caddie

•Huston's Rule of Negative Returns. The harder the swing, the shorter the shot. *Corollary Law of the Unworkable Hypothesis:* If your drive is short, you must hit the second shot twice as hard to make up the distance, your third shot must be three times as hard, and so forth.

> —Canadian humorist Mervyn J. Huston, in *Golf and Murphy's Law* (1981)

•Hutchinson's Reality. A man must be fed to play golf. It is ill going golfing on an empty interior.

> —Golf writer Horace Hutchinson (1859–1932)

I

•Ike's Advice to Golfers. When you are in any contest, you should work as if there were— to the very last minute—a chance to lose it. This is battle, this is politics, this is anything.
—Dwight D. Eisenhower

J

•J. Jose's First Principle of Golf. Do not believe in miracles, rely on them.
> —Rule found on a coffee mug emblazoned with assorted rules of life

•Jensen's Law. When you're hot, you're hot, and when you're not, everybody is watching.
> —Lynn Jensen, Littleton, Colorado. Created as general life law, but clearly true of golf. A corollary to Jensen's Law is that the closer you are to the clubhouse, the worse the shot.

•Jim Nasium's Law. In a large locker room, with hundreds of lockers, the few people using the facility at any one time will all be at their lockers and will be next to each other so that everybody is cramped.
> —Gary Neustadter, San Jose, California

•Johnson's Definition. A game in which you claim the privileges of age, and retain the playthings of childhood.

—Samuel Johnson

•Johnson's Percentage. [Based on the old adage that states that "the space occupied by a given tree is said to be 10 percent wood and 90 percent air."] A golf ball driven through the branches of a tree will hit the 10-percent wood 90 percent of the time, and the 90-percent air 10 percent of the time.

—R. D. Johnson, in the
Toronto Globe and Mail, from
Bob Norris

•Jones's Advice. (1) Play it as a game, regardless of what you score. (2) Don't worry about par. The practice of printing par figures is literally a mental hazard. (3) Enjoy your good shots and stay relaxed on the bad ones.
(4) Keep any gambling down to small stakes.
(5) Don't be ambitious. Why try shots that test champions when a small sacrifice will put you in the clear for a clean shot? (6) Don't expect miracles from pro lessons. Be content with small improvement from constant practice.
(7) Enjoy the surroundings. They're the loveliest of any game. (8) Enjoy your companions. They make the game.

—Titled "Jones' Way of Getting More from Golf," these eight points were made by Bobby Jones (1902–1971) and originally appeared in *Holiday* magazine in July 1946

•Jones's Confession. If I have any genius at all, it must be a genius for play! I love to play— I love fishing and hunting and trapshooting and ping-pong and chess and pool and billiards and driving a motor-car, and at times I love golf, when I can get the shots going somewhere near right. It seems I love almost any pursuit except work.

—Robert T. (Bobby) Jones, Jr., *The American Scrapbook* (1928)

•Jump's Discovery. Life is a lot like golf. You drive hard to get to the green and then you end up in the hole.

—Gary Jump, Bensenville, Illinois

K

•**Karras's Career Stat.** My best score ever is 103. But I've only been playing fifteen years.
> —Alex Karras, of pro football fame

•**Kavet's Driving Range Discovery.** The driving range is the sadistic relief center for golf. Here is where golfers line up to try to hit some poor unfortunate, locked in a steel cage built around an old jeep. The guy who picks up balls in this contraption is usually a former caddie who talked too much about his client's indiscretions of scoring—most golfers feel this punishment is too light.
> —Herbert I. Kavet, in his 1992 opus *Golf*

•**Kennedy's Explanation.** It is true that my predecessor did not object as I do to pictures of one's golfing skill in action. But neither, on the other hand, did he ever bean a Secret Service man.
> —John F. Kennedy, quoted in Bill Adler's *Kennedy Wit*

•Kevorkian Comforting Solution to Bad Golf. I'm going to walk up to Jack Nicklaus and tell him, "If you don't win, I'm here."

> —Dr. Jack Kevorkian, at the 1996 U.S. Open, quoted in *USA Today,* June 17, 1996

•Kibble's Golf Observation. The ball will hook toward the more difficult of two hazards.

> —Gary Kibble, Satellite Beach, Florida

•Knox's Big Stick Rule. The guys who are respected the most let their clubs do the talking.

> —Kenny Knox

•Koufax's Milestone. I've improved. Now I'm just terrible.

> —Baseball Hall of Famer Sandy Koufax, quoted by George Vecsey in *The Baseball Life of Sandy Koufax*

L

•**Lardner's Laws.** (1) The two easiest shots in golf are the fourth putt and the explosion shot off the tee. (2) If you hit a ball with a mashie, it will sometimes go further than if you miss it with a driver.

> —The first is from Ring Lardner as quoted in *Golf Is a Funny Game* by Ken Janke (1992), and the second comes from *For Golfers Only* (1965) by Vic Fredericks.

•**Lemon's Law of the Links.** If you think it's hard to meet new people, try picking the wrong golf ball.

> —Jack Lemon, *Sports Illustrated*, December 9, 1985

•**Linkert's Discovery.** A good golfer is a person who is able to laugh at himself in public and cries when he's alone.

> —Lo Linkert, in his 1993 work *Golf Fever* (Spectacle Lane Press)

•**Littler's Law.** Golf is not a game of great shots. It's a game of the most misses. The people who win make the smallest mistakes.

—Golfer Gene Littler, 1969

•**Locke's Lock.** You drive for show but putt for dough.

—Golfer Bobby Locke
(1917–1987)

M

•**Mandel's Dismissal.** Golf is a game with the soul of a 1956 Rotarian.

> —Bill Mandel, quoted in the Robert Byrne's *1,911 Best Things Anybody Ever Said*

•**Manion's Mantra.** Always aim at something you don't want to hit.

> —Steve Manion, Concord, Massachusetts, via Bob Skole

•**Marr's Advice.** Never bet with anyone you meet on the first tee who has a deep suntan, a 1-iron in his bag, and squinty eyes.

> —Dave Marr, former PGA champion, quoted in George Eberl's *Golf Is a Good Walk Spoiled* (1992), which is one of a number of a books to use Mark Twain's famous line as a title

•McCobb's Blessing. Golf is the strangest of games. There is no good argument for or against it. So let it be and he who plays it. And his widow and his orphaned children.
> —Gus McCobb, Chicago, Illinois

•Mead's List of Golf's Great Technological Advances. (1) The golf cart. (2) The telescoping retriever for scooping your ball, and others, out of bounds. (3) The suction cup that enables you to pick up your ball without bending over. (4) The cold-drinks cart that circulates around the course on hot days. (5) Television, which gives you the choice of watching golf rather than playing it.
> —William Mead, Bethesda, Maryland

•Melville's Revision. They talk of the dignity of work. Bosh. The dignity is in the leisure.
> —Herman Melville, who seemed to have been more interested in fishing than golf

•Metz's Rules of Golf for Good Players (Whose Scores Would Reflect Their True Ability if Only They Got an Even Break Once in a While). (1) On beginning play, as many balls as may be required to obtain a satisfactory result may be played from the first tee. Everyone recognizes a good player needs to "loosen up" but does not have time for the practice tee. (2) A ball sliced or hooked into the rough shall be lifted and placed in the fairway at a point equal to the distance it carried or rolled in the rough. Such veering right or left frequently results from friction between the face of the club and the cover of the ball, and the player should not be penalized for erratic behavior of the ball resulting from such uncontrollable mechanical phenomena. (3) A ball hitting a tree shall be deemed not to have hit the tree. Hitting a tree is simply bad luck and has no place in a scientific game. The player should estimate the distance the ball would have traveled if it had not hit the tree and play the ball from there, preferably from atop a nice firm tuft of grass. (4) There shall be no such thing as a lost ball. The missing ball is on or near the course somewhere and eventually will be found and pocketed by someone else. It thus becomes a stolen ball, and the player should not compound the felony by charging himself with a penalty stroke. (5) When played from a sand trap, a ball that does not clear the trap on being struck may be hit again on the roll without counting an extra stroke. In no case will more than two strokes be counted in playing from a trap, since it is only reasonable to assume that if the player had time to concentrate on his shot, instead of hurrying it so as not to delay his playing partners, he would be out in two. (6) If a putt passes over the hole without dropping, it is deemed to have dropped. The law of gravity holds that any object attempting to maintain a position in the atmosphere without something to support it must drop. The law of gravity supersedes the law of golf. (7) Same thing goes for a ball that stops at the brink of the hole and hangs there, defying gravity. You cannot defy the law. (8) Same thing goes for a ball that rims the cup. A ball should not go sideways. This violates the laws of physics. (9) A putt that stops close enough to the cup to inspire such comments as "You could blow it in" may be blown in. This rule does not apply if the ball is more than three inches from the hole, because no one wants to make a travesty of the game.

> —Donald A. Metz, Devon, Pennsylvania

•**Miller's Realization.** Serenity is knowing that your worst shot is going to be pretty good.

> —Golfer Johnny Miller

•Milne's Revelation. Golf is so popular simply because it is the best game in the world at which to be bad.
> —Author A. A. Milne
> (1882–1956), in his book *Not That It Matters*, (1919)

•Mollick's Rule of the Root. Avoid teeing off with parsnips—guys who quietly record their scores until after the 18th hole when they proclaim they've beaten you by a couple of strokes.
> —John J. Mollick,
> Fayetteville, Pennsylvania

•Morley's Conclusion. The ball is man's most disastrous invention, not excluding the wheel.
> —Actor Robert Morley
> (1908–1992)

•Morley's Distinction. The size of a man can be measured by the size of the thing that makes him angry.
> —J. K. Morley

•The Mulligan-Beard Biological Discovery. A tap-in is the larval stage of a hop-out.
> —From the 1993 work
> *Mulligan's Laws* by "Thomas

Mulligan" and edited by
Henry Beard

•**Murphy's Dictum.** Fishing was invented to
make golf seem interesting.
                    —Arthur J. Murphy, Chicago,
                    Illinois

•**Murray's Observation.** Golf is the most
over-taught and least-learned human endeavor.
If they taught sex the way they teach golf, the
race would have died out years ago.
                    —Columnist Jim Murray in
                    Golf magazine, 1989

N

•**Nicklaus's Conclusion.** Golf is not and never has been a fair game.
—Jack Nicklaus

•**19th Hole Observation.** The older I get, the better I used to be.
—Comment overheard by one of Bob Levey's *Washington Post* readers and reported in his column on April 16, 1986

•**Nixon's Trade-off.** By the time you get dressed, drive out there, play eighteen holes, and come home, you've blown seven hours. There are better things you can do with your time.
—President Richard M. Nixon

•**Norman's Declaration.** I owe a lot to my parents—especially my mother and father.
—Greg Norman (The Great White Shark)

•The North Carolina Tourist Council Boast.
"Famous mid-south resorts, including Pinehurst
and Southern Pines, where it is said that there
are more golf curses per square mile than any-
where else in the world . . ."

—From a state publicity
brochure, ca. 1958

O

•The Obligatory Politically Incorrect Frugal Scot's Response. "Great Scott, ye've holed in one!" "Ay, it saves the wear an' tear o' th' ball."

—Trad. and/or Anon.

• Offit's Observation. Golf courses are designed for the pros, while most of us are not. If they were designed for the majority, all of the hazards would be in the middle of the fairway.

—Morris W. Offit, Chairman, Offitbank, New York City

•O'Loughlin's Confession. I am so tense at times that I can hear the bees farting.

—Mick O'Loughlin, Irish pro in 1938 quoted in *Golf's Most Outrageous Quotes: An Official Bad Golfers Association Book* by Bruce Nash and Allan Zullo with Bill Hartigan

•**Orben's Warning.** You have to be a little suspicious of anyone who writes down his golf score and then wipes his fingerprints off the pencil. *Orben's Simile for Golfers:* Playing golf is a little like carving a turkey. It helps if you have your slice under control.
> —Comedy writer Bob Orben,
> Arlington, Virginia

P

•Palmer's Conclusion. It is contrary to nature for a man to say that he shot a lousy round. This is especially the case with a pro, who isn't supposed to shoot lousy rounds. So when he comes up with an embarrassing score, he can place the blame on one of two things. He can blame his body, claiming an injury to his wrist, his shoulder or his back. Or he can blame the course, pointing to poor maintenance, poor planning or poor location. It is easier to blame the course, because if you claim an injury, and come back the following week to win a tournament with an 18-under-par score, it gets a little sticky.

> —Arnold Palmer, in a *TV Guide* interview March 22, 1975

•Palmer's Percentage. Once the fundamentals of golf are mastered, about 90 percent of the game depends on judgement and attitude. On the pro tournament level, I'm inclined to raise the figure to 95 percent.

> —Arnold Palmer in his book *Situation Golf* (1970)

•**Peterson's Law.** A bad golf shot always travels far enough to land in more trouble.
—Leroy A. Peterson,
Bartlesville, Oklahoma

Pillow Talk

Mottoes embroidered on pillows for golfers are a staple in golf catalogs, pro shops, and in golf stores around the world.

Whether or not people actually buy these— $29.00 a pillow is the common price—is another question, because they force the issue of whether or not people are comfortable sitting on revealed truth. They probably do sell, because golfers are constantly looking for a comforting line, and hence, we tend to put our mottoes on cushions rather than bumper stickers or T-shirts. The words are our staff and pillow, and comfort us when we lie back to watch golf on television.

Here are a few choice golfer's cushions from recent years (usually written in green on a white background and framed in green and gold trim).

⚲

HE WHO HAS THE FASTEST CART NEVER
HAS A BAD LIE.

I ONCE GAVE UP GOLF. IT WAS THE MOST
TERRIFYING WEEKEND OF MY LIFE.

MISSING! GOLFER-HUSBAND AND DOG.
REWARD FOR DOG.

GOLF IS NOT A MATTER OF LIFE AND
DEATH. IT'S MUCH MORE
IMPORTANT THAN THAT.

I'M NOT OVER THE HILL.
I'M JUST ON THE BACK NINE.

OLD GOLFERS NEVER DIE;
THEY JUST LOSE THEIR BALLS.

I'D RATHER BE GOLFING.

WORK IS FOR PEOPLE WHO DON'T HAVE
TIME FOR GOLF.

•**Plato's Answer.** What, then, is the right way
of living? Life must be lived as a play, playing
certain games, making sacrifices; singing and
dancing, then a man will be able to propitiate
the gods, and defend himself against his ene-
mies, and win the contest.
—Plato

•Player's Description. The ideal build for a golfer would be strong hands, big forearms, thin neck, big thighs, and a flat chest. He'd look like Popeye.

> —Gary Player, on the perfect golfer

•Player's Razor. They say Sam Snead is a natural golfer. But if he didn't practice, he'd be a natural bad golfer.

> —Gary Player, on the importance of practice

•Plimpton's Correlation. There exists an inverse correlation between the size of the ball and the quality of the writing about the game in which it is used.

> —The correlation was written by George Plimpton, who explained, "There are superb books about golf, very good books about baseball, not very many good books about basketball, and no good books on beachballs." This goes a long way toward answering the question of why is it that so much else that is written on golf is so literate, simple, and sublime.

How can a game that produces so many curses on the course inspire so many insights, blessings, and bon mots—or is it bons mot—off the course?

•**Pollard's Definition.** A game where the ball lies poorly and the player well.

—John Garland Pollard, editor of the *Connotary* and governor of Virginia from 1930 to 1934

•**Powers's Assumption.** Showing up at a golf course as an adult with your own clubs is like showing up for a final exam. It's assumed you know something about the subject.

—John Powers, in *B.G.* magazine, October 2, 1994

_Q_

Question Worth Asking Another Golfer, The Only

If you could create a foursome with three other individuals—living or dead—whom would you pick?

> —This is a traditional question. Here are two sample answers:
>
> 1. Jerry Ford, a faith healer, and a paramedic. (Bob Hope reported this as the selection of President Gerald R. Ford in Carol Mann's _The 19th Hole_ (1992).
>
> 2. Jesus Christ, Arnold Palmer, and Bob Hope (Lee Trevino, in _Fore Play, the Very Best of Playboy's Classic Golf Humor,_ edited by Michelle Urry (1995)

R

Revised Proverbs

A collection of golfing maxims and proverbs, mostly by the two great authors of golfing wisdom Anon. and Trad.:

- A player on foot has no standing on the course.
- A straight line is the shortest distance between two putts.
- All is fair in love and golf.
- Any golfer can be devout on a rainy Sabbath.
- Eat, drink, and be merry, for tomorrow you may be off your game again.
- Golf is the only thing that depreciates above par.
- Golf is the roughest distance between two points.
- Golfers come and golfers go, but mostly the latter.
- Hell hath no fury like a bunkered dub.
- If all the golfers in the world were laid end to end, they would lie indefinitely.
- If at first you don't succeed, try looking at the ball.

• If at first you do succeed, try to hide your astonishment.

• If you are topping the ball, try teeing it with the other side up.

• If you drink, don't drive. Don't even putt.

• If you see two people talking, the one who isn't yawning is the golfer.

• If you swing your club like an ax, it is only natural that you should strike a tree.

• It is a wise golf course that knows its own par.

• It's a poor rule that doesn't work your way.

• Many think golf is for the rich, but this is belied by the fact that there are millions of poor players.

• Money doesn't grow on tees (for those who "invest" in a new set of clubs).

• Nothing handicaps you so much in golf as honesty.

• Old golfers never die—they simply lose their drive.

• Only the brave deserve the fairway.

• The course of true golf never ran true.

• The proof is in the putting.

• The real test of golf—and life—is not keeping out of the rough, but getting out after we are in.

• There is many a slip 'twixt the tee and the cup.

• There is nothing like a good sand trap to make you forget your other troubles.

• Two can live as cheaply as one can play golf.

•When you are playing golf, nothing counts like your opponent.

•**Rockefeller's Clerical Observation.** Golf courses are the best places to observe ministers. But none of them are above cheating a bit.

> —John D. Rockefeller, quoted by William Manchester in *A Rockefeller Family Portrait* (1959)

•**Rogers Reminder.** Rail-splitting produced an immortal president in Abraham Lincoln; but golf, with 29,000 courses, hasn't produced even a good A-number-1 congressman.

> —Will Rogers (1878–1935), who was probably unaware of the fact that three of the Scottish golfers who won the British Open between 1883 and 1902 were plasterers: Willie Fernie, Jack Burns, and Sandy Herd. Rogers also once remarked: "Golf is a wonderful exercise. You can stand on your feet for hours watching somebody else putt," and he also informed us, "The income tax has

made more liars out of the
American people than golf
has."

•**Rooke's Rule.** Nothing is as simple as it
seems.

—William Rooke, Anaheim,
California

•**Roosevelt's Razor.** It is of far more importance that a man shall play something himself,
even if he plays it badly, than that he shall go
with hundreds of companions to see someone
else play well.

—President Theodore
Roosevelt

•**Dr. Rosse's Razor.** Instead of dividing
mankind, as some mathematicians do, into two
classes, namely those who read analytical geom-
etry and those who do not, it is more appropri-
ate to divide them into those who play golf and
those who do not, or as an enthusiastic devotee
to golf might put it, those who are long drivers
and those who are not.

—Irving C. Rosse, from the
August 6, 1898, *Journal of the
American Medical Association.*
In his paper "Golf from a
Neurological View-Point,"

Rosse promoted the medical benefits of the game. To quote the good doctor: "In addition to the unconscious vigor of body and mind imparted by golf, the social amenities arising therefrom are of unquestionable thera-peutic value, since the genial influences of the game by expanding the ideas tend to promote the good fellowship that comes from diversion and sensuous amusement, and by oiling the wheels of life, so to speak, makes them go on with rattling glee."

•The Royal Remark. Golf always makes me so damned angry.

—King George V of England, quoted by Peter Ross in the British *Sunday Referee*, December 28, 1938. George's comment suggests the possi-ble origin of the opinion that "golf is a royal pain in the ass." Clearly, golf is extremely frustrating even to monarchs, as the ball refuses to succumb to the royal swing and putt. Listen to Princess Anne: "Golf seems to me an arduous way to go for a walk. I prefer to take the dogs out." Dogs and horses obey, cats and golf balls do not.

The "Rules of Golf" Revised

Almost twenty years ago, M. Mack Earle, then of Baltimore, sent the Murphy Center a collection of revised golfing rules, which were crudely mimeographed on the stationery of the SOO Line Railroad Company. The Director had not seen them before this, nor has he ever seen them again. If only they were so. Lacking anything else to go on, the Director attributes them, once again, to the indefatigable Anon. and Trad.

(1) A ball rolling or flying into a bunker or sand trap may be played, if the player feels he is in need of the practice or enjoys that kind of thing. But no strokes other than the first one made in the bunker shall be counted against said player. Should the ball fail to emerge after the making of this first stroke, the faulty design of the bunker is deemed aptly demonstrated, and the skill of the player should not be penalized for a defect in construc-

tion over which he has no control

(2) In order to spare the valuable turf of the Course and to protect club property when teeing the ball up in the Fairway, the player must hereafter employ small wooden pegs or tees. Should the stroke played from one of these wooden pegs result in the player finding himself in difficulties, he shall have the right to examine both the peg and the consistency of the ground into which it was thrust. Should a defect be apparent in either, he may play the stroke again since the purpose of the game is to eliminate all mechanical and extraneous factors so the genuine beauty of the sport shall be permitted to flourish.

(3) All shots that curve into the rough on the right or left shall be returned to the Fairway at the farthest point of flight or roll, since this curvature is frequently an uncontrollable mechanical phenomenon resulting from friction between the face of the club and the cover of the ball and results in it landing in areas that no player in his right mind may wish to enter for the sake of the play.

(4) A ball striking a tree while in flight shall be deemed not to have struck a tree unless the player making the stroke declares that he was deliberately aiming for it. In this case, play shall cease momentarily while his partners congratulate him on his marksmanship. But if the

player attests in good faith that it was in no sense his intention to strike the tree, then it is obviously a piece of bad luck that has no place in a scientific game. No penalty shall accrue to the player, who is thereupon permitted to estimate the distance his ball would have traveled, but no more than half the distance to the goal line, or two bases.

(5) There is no such thing as a lost ball. The ball is somewhere on the course and will be picked up eventually and pocketed by someone other than the owner, therefore becoming not a lost ball, but a stolen ball. A player suffering a stolen ball shall be entitled to cries of sympathy from his fellow players, who shall crowd around him importuning him not to compound the felony by charging himself with the loss of a stroke. Upon returning to the clubhouse, the player shall apply to the professional for restitution of the stolen article, since this official always has a large supply of balls on hand.

(6) In arriving at a judgment on whether or not ground is under repair for purpose of lifting a ball unpleasantly situated without penalty, the player shall toss a coin. If it falls, the ground may be deemed under repair.

(7) A ball that rims the cup and stays out shall be deemed to have dropped, since the occurrence shall be held contrary to the laws of gravitation, which supersede the rules of golf and are

therefore illegal. The same rule shall be in force
for balls that pass over the hole and stay out,
since it is a well-known fact that any object
attempting to maintain its position in atmosphere with nothing to support it must drop.

(8) A ball putted that reaches the brink of the
cup and hangs there for want of a half or quarter turn to cause it to drop shall be deemed to
have made that turn and duly dropped. This
providing the player has indicated by bodily
contortions and gestures that he was genuinely
desirous of this result. For since the player has
thus indicated that he has made a diligent and
accurate putt and it is not through any lack of
desire on his part that the ball failed to complete its journey, it shall be so scored. Likewise,
to eliminate complaints to the effect that the
ball was "so close you could have blown it in,"
the player in such case shall place himself
behind the ball and blow. If the ball drops,
it shall be deemed to have been holed out
properly.

•**Dr. Rush's Explanation.** He who puts the
ball into a given number of holes with the
fewest strokes gets the prize. A man would live
ten years longer for this exercise once or twice a
week.

—Benjamin Rush, in

Sermons to Gentlemen Upon Temperance and Exercise, the first book in which golf in the United States is mentioned. Rush may be best known as one of the signers of the Declaration of Independence.

S

•**The Scott-Cousins Rules for Playing Golf in Comfort.** (1) Leave home in plenty of time. (2) Decide how many holes to play—and stick to it. (3) Take sufficient time for lunch and refuse to be rushed out afterwards. (4) Play foursomes whenever possible.

> —Tom Scott and Geoffrey Cousins, from their book *The Wit of Golf* (1972)

Shakespeare the Golfer

"Human nature is so funny, it is such a thousand pities that neither Aristotle nor Shakespeare was a golfer. There is no other game that strips the soul so naked."
> —H. G. Hutchinson

Although Hutchinson and others have lamented that Shakespeare did not play, there is, however, some significant evidence to suggest that the Bard was in fact a golfer, and allusions to the game are salted throughout his works.

First there is the evidence from *A Midsummer Night's Dream* pointing to the inescapable conclusion that Shakespeare's own dream was a midafternoon round at the Avon CC. The evidence?

But yet you draw not iron . . .
—Act 2, Scene 1
Nor doth this wood lack worlds of company.
—Act 2, Scene 1
Thou drivest me past the bounds . . .
—Act 3, Scene 2
It goes not forward, doth it?
—Act 4, Scene 2

The clincher is this line, which can only be interpreted as a reminder from the great man to himself to keep his head down:

. . . so sanded, and their heads are hung . . .
—Act 4, Scene 1

The allusions are everywhere, from mustering determination on the links:

. . . bear-like, I must fight the course.
—*Macbeth*, Act 5, Scene 7

to testing the winds before a drive:

I should still be plucking the grass where sits the wind.
—*Merchant of Venice*, Act 1, Scene 1

to a rough putting green:
Uneven is the course, I like it not.
> —*Romeo and Juliet,* Act 4,
> Scene 1

to a bad partner:
A poor player that struts and frets.
> —*Macbeth,* Act 5, Scene 5

to a caddie in the way:
Stand aside, good bearer.
> —*Love's Labor's Lost,* Act 4,
> Scene 1

to the nature of golf itself:
Certain issues strokes must arbitrate.
> —*Macbeth,* Act 5, Scene 4

to the golfer who has driven past the green:
You have shot over.
> —*Henry V,* Act 3, Scene 7

to an opponent who has missed all of the hazards:
Was there ever man had such luck!
> —*Cymbeline,* Act 2, Scene 1

to a consistent swing (perhaps the Bard's own):
In my school-days, when I had lost one shaft,

I shot his fellow of the self-same flight
The self-same way with more advised watch
To find the other forth; and by adventuring both,
I oft found both.

> —*The Merchant of Venice,* Act
> 1, Scene 1

Of course, the most compelling line is the one the great playwright penned the day he realized that his golfing season was over: "Now is the winter of our discontent."

(Help on this link between Shakespeare and the links appears in *On the Green* by Samuel J. Looker, London [1922], *The Pro and Con of Golf* by Alexander H. Revell [1915], *The Golf Joke Book* by Seymour Dunn [1953], and *How to Break 90 Before You Reach It* by Sidney "Steve" Brody [1967], which contain even more proof.)

Signs, Rules, and Committee Postings Reportedly Found on Clubhouse Bulletin Boards and in Pro Shops Worldwide

---

EVERYTHING FOR THE GOLFER . . .
EXCEPT PROFANITY.

> —Sign in a Westchester
> County, New York, pro shop
> according to Don January

and Al Carrell in their *Golf Is a Funny Game* (1967)

IF A BALL COMES TO REST IN DANGEROUS PROXIMITY TO A HIPPOPOTAMUS OR CROCODILE, ANOTHER BALL MAY BE DROPPED AT A SAFE DISTANCE, NO NEARER THE HOLE, WITHOUT PENALTY.

—Local Rule, Nyanza Club, British East Africa, 1950

MEMBERS WILL REFRAIN FROM PICKING UP LOST BALLS UNTIL THEY HAVE STOPPED ROLLING.

——From a Scottish course, according to B. C. Forbes in *499 Scottish Stories* (1945)

YOU CANNOT GROUND YOUR CLUB IN ADDRESSING THE BALL, OR MOVE ANYTHING, HOWEVER LOOSE OR DEAD IT MAY BE.

—Royal Selanger Golf Club, built on an ancient Chinese burial ground near Kuala Lumpur

⛳⛳⛳

From a Committee Minute:
The condition of the draught beer, which had

been the subject of some complaints from members, was looked into throughly by the Committee. It was decided the complaints were groundless, for although the first pint or two tended to be cloudy, the beer was excellent right down to the bottom of the barrel.

> —Tom Scott and Geoffrey Cousins in *The Wit of Golf* (1972), who also report this committee minute posted somewhere in the British Isles:

IT IS EASIER TO REPLACE THE TURF THAN TO RETURF THE PLACE.

•**Snead's Advice to Golf Widows.** When your husband comes home with cockleburs in the cuffs of his pants, don't ask him what his score was.

> —Sam Snead, quoted in the *Reader's Digest*, November 1987

•**Snead's Distinction between Baseball and Golf.** When we hit a foul ball, we've gotta get out there and play it.

> —"Slamming Sammy" Snead

to Ted Williams, who along with his Red Sox teammates were ribbing him about golf's inferiority to baseball.

•**Sneddon's Reminder.** Remember, you can always find a golf ball when you are not looking for it by being where you wouldn't be if you were looking for it. *Sneddon's Conclusion:* When you see two golfers striding quickly, single file, off the last green, it's the one in front that's mad. *Sneddon's Warning:* Fool around with your work too long and the first thing you know, your golf game will go to pieces. *Sneddon's Seeming Paradox of the Golfer:* There are two periods of extreme dissatisfaction in [the golfer's] life: before he takes up golf and after he takes up golf.

—Richard Sneddon, from his 1941 classic *The Golf Stream.* Sneddon was a golf humorist who was the first to acknowledge that the funniest things in golf "must be seen to be appreciated, and can never quite be told."

•**Southern's Rule.** If you want them to play your course—don't put rocks on the green!

—Terry Southern, in his
novel *The Magic Christian*
(1960)

•Statistical Truths of Golf, Three. (1) 13.9
percent of the people play golf—or is it 13.9 percent of the golfers? (2) The odds on making a
hole in one are 14,937 against on any given
hole. (3) The 17th hole at the Black Mountain
Club in North Carolina is 745 yards; few of us
have played it, but on many days at least one
hole on any given course feels that long.
—Various sources

•Swarbrick's Saw. Golf is not a particularly
natural game. Like sword-swallowing, it has to
be learned.

—Brian Swarbrick, 1973,
quoted in *Golf Is a Funny
Game* by Ken Janke (1992)

T

Tee Talk

A modest collection of golf T-shirt mottoes, which most golfers wear only on days when other events conspire to keep them off the links.

⛳

AGED TO PARFECTION

⛳

EAT, SLEEP & GOLF

⛳

I HATE GOLF
I HATE GOLF
"NICE SHOT"
I LOVE GOLF . . .

⛳

I ONLY PLAY GOLF ON DAYS THAT
END IN Y.

⛳

IT TAKES A LOT OF BALLS TO GOLF THE
WAY I DO.

⛳

WHERE IS THE FIRST TEE AND WHAT IS
THE COURSE RECORD?

⛳

IF THERE'S NO GOLF IN HEAVEN,
I'M NOT GOING.

⛳

GOLF IS HOW I ROUGH IT.

•**Thranghan's Law of Playing Through.**
The game of a golfer playing through falls apart
at a speed equal to the speed with which he
overtook the group he is passing.

> —Person named Thranghan,
> from Dick Brooks's *The*
> *Offensive Golfer* (1963)

•**Townshend's Summary of All Good Advice
on Hitting a Golf Ball.** Keep your eye on the
ball, slow back, start the club up with the wrists,
left wrist hollow not arched, grip with the fin-
gers, grip tight with the left, grip tighter in the
down swing, upper arms near the body, left hip

well round towards the ball, left shoulder well down to the ball, backbone the axis of swing, head as still as possible, follow through with the arms, hands away and left foot at finish firm on the ground.

> —From *Inspired Golf* by R. B. Townshend (1921), who added that there are scores more. Townshend said all of these tips recalled the predicament of the unfortunate insect with her hundred legs:

The centipede was happy quite
Until the toad in fun
Said, "Pray which leg goes after which?"
And worked her mind to such a pitch
She lay distractcd in the ditch
Considering how to run.

•Trevino's Rule. There's only two things in the world you gotta do with your head down— golf and praying.

> —Lee Trevino, quoted in David Guiney's, *The Dunlop Book of Golf* (1973)

•Trevino's Theological Advice on Lightning. Hold up a 1-iron and walk. Even God can't hit a 1 iron.

—Lee Trevino (who was once
hit by lightning while playing
a round of golf,) when asked
how other players could
avoid a similar fate

W

•Warning to Lunar Golfers. Warmest congratulations to all of you on your great achievement and safe return. Please refer to Rules of Golf section on etiquette, paragraph 6—"Before leaving a bunker, player should carefully fill up all holes made by him therein."

> —Telegram from the Royal and Ancient Club to astronaut Alan Shepard, who commanded *Apollo 14* in February 1971 and who— between other chores on the moon's surface—hit the highest golf shot ever made. It was a 6-iron shot, and the ball went about 700 yards.

•Wells's Law. The uglier a man's legs are, the better he plays golf.

> —English novelist and historian H. G. Wells (1866–1946), in *Bealby* (1915)

•Wells's Rule. Never trust a golfer whose friends call him Pele.

—Stephen B. Wells, New
Canaan, Connecticut

•Lord Wellwood's Bid for the Women's Golf Hall of Shame. We venture to suggest 70 or 80 yards as the average limit of a drive advisedly, not because we doubt a lady's power to take a longer drive but because that cannot well be done without raising the club above the shoulder. We do not presume to dictate but must observe that the postures and gestures requisite for a full swing are not particularly graceful when the player is clad in female dress.

—From a small volume on
golf, published in 1890 and
recalled in the 1973 *Dunlop
Book of Golf* by David Guiney

•White's Prescription. A man ought to have a doctor's prescription to be allowed to use a golf cart.

—Dr. Paul Dudley White,
heart specialist

•Why Golf Is Better than Fishing. (1) A golfer doesn't have to show anything to prove it. (2) The golfer never brags about the one that got away. (3) You need no license. (4) You need only one hook, and you set it on the first tee you ever play and never have to replace it as long as you live.

>   —Anon. and Trad.

•**Williams's Sartorial Observation.** Golf is the only game in which middle-class, middle-aged guys can dress like pimps.

>   —Robin Williams, quoted in
>   the Chicago *Tribune*, April 21,
>   1996

•**Willis's Rule of Golf.** You can't lose an old golf ball.

>   —Television personality John
>   Willis

•**Wilson's Definition.** A lot of walking, broken up by disappointment and bad arithmetic.
—Columnist Earl Wilson

•**Wilson's Discovery.** A game in which one endeavors to control a ball with implements ill-adapted for the purpose.
—Woodrow Wilson. A similar discovery was attributed to Winston Churchill on BBC Radio by Alistair Cooke on December 27, 1974: "Golf is a game whose aim is to hit a very small ball into an even smaller hole, with weapons singularly ill-designed for the purpose." In fact, the quote can be found in the August 6, 1898, issue of the *Journal of the American Medical Association* and an article by Irving C. Rosse titled "Golf from a Neurological View-Point," which opens with this line: "Long before the Columbian rediscovery of America our hardy Caledonian ancestry amused themselves by playing the royal and ancient game

which has been defined as 'the putting of little balls into little holes with instruments very ill adapted to the purpose.' "

Wodehouse's Three Best Golfing Lines

P. G. Wodehouse (1881–1975) the English writer, created some of the better lines on the royal and ancient game in his golf writing. Three choice examples:

1. "The least thing upset him on the links. He missed short putts because of the uproar of butterflies in the adjoining meadow."

2. "Few things draw two men together more surely than a mutual inability to master golf, coupled with an intense and ever-increasing love of the game."

3. " 'The only way,' I said to Alexander, of really finding out a man's true character is to play golf with him. In no other walk of life does the cloven hoof so quickly display itself. I employed a lawyer for years, until one day I saw him kick his ball out of a heel mark. I removed my business from his charge next morning." (From "The Acid Test.")

•Wordsworth's Definition. A day spent in a round of strenuous idleness.

> —William Wordsworth
> (1770–1850), English poet, in
> *The Prelude,* his book on his
> boyhood

X-Y-Z

• **Youngman's Historic Parallel.** I played Civil War golf. I went out in 61 and came back in 65.

> —Henny Youngman, quoted in Carol Mann's *The 19th Hole* (1992)

• **Zaharias's Constants.** (1) Winning has always meant much to me, but winning friends has meant the most. (2) That little ball won't move until you hit it, and there's nothing you can do for it after it has gone.

> —Babe Didrikson Zaharias (1914–1976)—some say the best all-around athlete, male or female, to play professional golf

• **Zorn's Snappy Comeback Lines to Rude Golfers.** (1) Don't let my putt interrupt your conversation. (2) Where did you learn to whisper, in a sawmill?

> —Robert E. Zorn, from his 1993 book *Real Golfers Don't Take Mulligans*

Special Bonus Sections

Toasts, Jokes, Etc.—Equipment for the 19th Hole

These items should come in handy at the end of a round.

Toast #1

Here's to the man with club in hand,
Here's to the king of bogey land;
Here's to thc clubs with outlandish names,
And here's to GOLF the game of games!
> —*The Father Gander Golf Book* (1909)

Toast #2

To brag little;
To show well.
To improve gently given luck.
To pay up,
To own up
And to shut up if beaten
These are the virtues of the sporting man.

—From *The American Golfer*
magazine (ca. 1910)

Toast #3

May your balls, as they fly and whiz through the air,
Knock down the blue devils, dull sorrow and care.
May your health be preserved, with strength active and bold,
Long traverse the green, and forget to grow old.
> —From a letter written by
> Henry Callender, secretary of
> the Royal Blackheath Club,
> and its captain in 1790, 1801,
> and 1807

Toast #4

May you live long enough to shoot your age.

Ecumenical Joke (fill in the blanks)

The truant _____ (priest, minister, rabbi) was playing an otherwise deserted course at the crack of dawn on _____ (Easter, Yom Kippur, other), hoping to sneak in a few quick holes. From the first tee, he furtively looked around and drove more than 400 yards

onto the green and right into the cup! He shook
an angry fist at the sky. "My very first hole in
one—and now whom can I tell?"

St. Peter Joke #1

St. Peter challenged God to a heavenly golf
match, and after Peter hit his tee shot close to
the pin and God sliced badly into the rough, the
twosome started hiking down the fairway.
Suddenly a squirrel picked up the Lord's golf
ball and darted away, only to be grasped by a
huge eagle, which carried the little animal high
into the sky. Dark clouds then filled the air as a
thunderbolt struck the bird, causing it to release
the squirrel, which, in turn, dropped the ball
onto the green, where it bounced several times
and rolled into the cup. "Damn it!" cried the
exasperated saint. "Are you going to screw
around or play golf."

St. Peter Joke #2

All men are mortal. Thus golfers, like the rest,
have to die and go on to their eternal destiny.
One devotee of the game had become such a
fanatic that when he was asked by St. Peter to
give an account of himself he replied shortly,
"Golf. I have devoted the whole of my life to
that; nothing else ever mattered."

The great keeper took him along until they came to the most luscious fairways and greens the golfer had ever dreamed of.

"Here you are," said the saint, "your heaven."

Delighted, the golfer set about opening the celestial bag of clubs included in the reward. "But you've forgotten to put any balls in," he complained.

"Not forgotten," said Peter. "They are not included."

"Hell!" exploded heaven's newcomer.

"Precisely," answered Peter.

St. Peter Joke #3

An ardent golfer is met by St. Peter and immediately blurts out that he has lived a good and moral life but the moment of his last breath he took the name of the Lord in vain.

St. Peter cocked an eyebrow and asked the golfer to tell his story.

"Well, sir, I was playing the course at Pebble Beach for the first time in my life, and as I began the 18th hole I realized that I was not only playing one of the great courses on earth but that if I could finish that last hole with a par four I would break 70 for the first time in my life."

"How was your drive?" asked the man of God.

"Superb," said the golfer. "Only, it landed in a

slight depression and I had to hit it smartly to get it near the green."

"And then what happened, my son?"

"Well, I landed in the trap and for my third stroke blasted it out to within two feet of the cup."

St. Peter looked at the golfer and shrieked: "Don't tell me . . . don't tell me. You missed the goddamn putt."

Glossary of Important Golfing Terms

The reader's enjoyment of this work will be
greater if he or she is familiar with the mean-
ings of the unusual terms used. Like almost
everything else in this book, the author relies
heavily on the cerebral heavy lifting of others to
come up with these definitions—all [terms not
contributed to the Murphy Center] are credited.

Ace. Mocking term of endearment, as in,
"Hey, ace, how did you manage to hit two trees
and a Canada goose in just one shot?"

Act of God. Describing a great drive or long,
difficult, and successful putt by an opponent.
Contrast with *skill:* Describing a great drive or
long, difficult, and successful putt by one's self.

Addressing the ball. Formal term for what a
player says to the ball after it ducks to avoid
being hit by the club head. (Fred Beck, in *To
Hell With Golf*) In the words of Art Carney—in
the role of Ed Norton—to address the ball is to
say, "Hello, ball."

Amateur. Any golfer in a slow foursome just
ahead. (Lawrence Larier, in *Golf and Be
Damned*)

Approach. (1) Shot intended for the green.
(2) Line uttered on or near a golf course; to wit:
　—Shall we play for twenty bucks a hole just

to make it interesting? On second thought, let's make that fifty.

—You ladies/gentlemen down here for the whole weekend all by yourselves?

Athlete's foot. The only athletic part of a golfer. (Tom Carey, from his book *Teed Off*)

Back nine. That half of the course on which you vow you will do better, but won't. (Art Rosenbaum, from his February 1963 *San Francisco Chronicle* column)

Ball. (1) Small, round object usually found in the deep woods and the only thing that smiles at you when you find it. (2) That which you are always standing too close to—after you hit it.

Bogey. (1) Par. (2) The star of *Casablanca.*

Break. In putting, your ball always breaks away from the cup. (Art Rosenbaum, from his February 1963 *San Francisco Chronicle* column)

Bunker. (1) Horrendous place. Hitler committed suicide in one. (Anon.) (2) Also, "a bogey golfer trying to explain how close he came to breaking par." (Fred Beck, from *To Hell with Golf,* 1956)

Casual water. Any temporary accumulation of water that is not one of the ordinary and recognized hazards of the course. This includes melted ice cubes. (*Fun in the Rough,* edited by Howard Gill, 1957)

Curve of the earth. Putting hazard.

Divot. (1) A hunk of the ground torn from

the course, on your shot, which inevitably travels farther than your ball. The first dozen or so should he replaced. Beyond that, the golfer should be replaced. (2) A flying carpet.

Driving range. A cunningly contrived trap. It attracts innocent nongolfers the way bright lights attract moths. Each tee is a tiny stage upon which the complete novice may strut and prance. An ever-present gallery of spectators, folks who don't know a duck hook from a swan, is there to watch and marvel at the shots that slice out into the darkness. (Joe James, *So You're Taking Up Golf,* 1965)

Dub. One who misses a shot with ease—as in, "easy dubs it." (Art Rosenbaum, from his February 1963 *San Francisco Chronicle* column)

Duffer. All of us.

Eagle. Also called "Iggle." Almost extinct on most courses and a rare member of the bird family. (Joe James, in *Kill It Before It Moves,* 1961)

Fairway. A green but largely uninhabited strip of turf running from tee to green.

Foot and mouth disease. Golfer's illness causing in victim bouts of swearing followed by kicking. (Trad. again, who is Anon.'s long-suffering partner)

Fore. (1) Futile cry informing the person in front of you that he or she has 1/119,765 of a second before being hit by the ball. (2) A shriek of triumph uttered by a player when his ball strikes a member of the slow foursome ahead. (Richard Sneddon, in *The Golf Stream*, 1941) (3) Golfing equivalent of an air-raid siren—lie flat, face down, with hands covering organs of choice.

Gimmie. An agreement between two losers who can't putt. (columnist Jim Bishop, from his April 1977 syndicated columns containing his multiparted golfer's lexicon)

"Give me a seven." A bid to accept a seven when one has committed $7 + n$—i.e., any number from 8 to ∞.

Golf bag. In the book *Post Humour* (1956), C. P. Donnel, Jr., gives this definition: "Bulky container, of paradoxical weight properties: one is too heavy for a 200-pound adult male seeking exercise; two are considered the correct burden for a 120-pound child."

Golf ball. (1) A stationary object which does not move until you hit it, therefore, as stated by British writer Patrick Campbell in his book *How to Become a Scratch Golfer*, "obviating all danger of being tackled or struck, or of having to run after it." (2) The ball used in playing the game of golf is called a "golf ball." It is white, dimpled like a bishop's knees, and is the size of small mandarin oranges or those huge pills which vets blow down the throats of constipated cart-horses. (Frank Muir, in his essay "Golf in a Nutshell," which appears in Peter Alliss's and Mike Seabrook's *One Over Par*, 1992)

Golf cart. Device that has largely displaced the caddie because it cannot count or criticize.

Golf course. (1) A tract of land where the people in front of you are always much slower than those behind you. (2) A ball mall.

Golfer. (1) A gardener digging up somebody else's lawn. (*Changing Times* magazine) (2) One who yells "fore," takes six, and puts down five. (3) One who can express his or her thoughts to a tee.

Golf pro. A crack putt.

Golf terms. The most common are unprintable and often hyphenated.

Green. (1) Grassy area just behind the sand traps. (Joe James, in *Kill It Before It Moves*, 1961) (2) Smooth, closely mowed area where you four-putt. (*How to Give Up Golf* by Joe James, 1970) (3) A far-off oasis featured by an alien flag on a stick. Never-never land. (columnist Jim Bishop, from his April 1977 syndicated columns containing his own golfer's lexicon) (4) Meeting place for slicers and hookers. (Art Rosenbaum, from his February 1963 *San Francisco Chronicle* column)

Handicap. (1) Something that age is no. (Richard Sneddon, in *The Golf Stream,* 1941) (2) Explained by this anecdote in Philip Ziegler's *Diana Cooper* (1981): " 'What is your handicap?' Lady Cunard asked Lord Castlerosse on the golf course. 'Drink and debauchery,' he answered sadly but truthfully."

Hazard. (1) Listening to stroke-by-stroke descriptions of interminable matches.
(2) Having to sympathize with habitual victims of "lucky" and/or "unethical" opponents.

Head. Portion of golfer that comes up just before ball is struck. (Joe James in *Kill It Before It Moves,* 1961)

Heel print. A small depression designated by fate to catch every shot you hit into the sand. (Grantland Rice and Clare Briggs, in *The Duffer's Handbook of Golf*)

Hook. A sharp left turn, usually made while driving. (Lawrence Larier, in *Golf and Be Damned,* 1954)

Improvement. Missing the ball closer than before.

Irons. (1) Club-like devices used primarily to mow down large swaths of grass, to destroy golf balls, and to attract lightning. (Tom Carey, from *Teed Off*) (2) What most golfers should be put into.

It'll play. "Your partner's cheerful comment after you hook, slice, fade or drive into the woods. It is synonymous with "won't hurcha." (columnist Jim Bishop, from his April 1977 lexicon)

Lie. Position of the ball after it has been hit. A couplet from J. E. Schrite's 1934 work *Divots for Dubs*:

The "lie of the ball," is the place which it selects, in an effort to avoid being hit.

Links. Series of small greens joined together by connecting fairways, all of which lead inevitably back to the clubhouse and a further series of stories, joined together by connecting falsehoods. (Lawrence Larier, in *Golf and Be Damned*, 1954)

Locker room. Sanctuary for ugly nudists. (columnist Jim Bishop, from his April 1977 lexicon)

Low clouds. Putting hazard.

Maniac. Any player in the group behind you playing faster than you would like. (Tom Carey, from *Teed Off*)

Marker. A disk placed a foot nearer the hole than the ball. (columnist Jim Bishop, from his April 1977 lexicon)

Mulligan. A thieving second shot employed by golfers to prove that the first one was no mistake. (Anon.)

Nineteenth hole. This couplet from Richard Armour's *Golf Is a Four-Letter Word:*

N is for nineteenth, the hole that's the best,
And the reason some golfers play all of the rest.

1-iron. Tom Scott and Geoffrey Cousins, in *The Wit of Golf* (1972), define it this way: "The one-iron is almost unplayable. You keep it in your bag the way you keep a Dostoyevsky novel in your bookcase—with the vague notion that you will try it some day. In the meantime it impresses your friends."

Penalty. Reward for going out of bounds.

Playing through. The custom of allowing a faster group of golfers to move through your group. On occasion a group will ask to play through, as in: "Hate to bother you all, but one of our foursome has just been bitten by a rattlesnake."

Pressure. Playing for ten dollars when you don't have a dime in your pocket. (Lee Trevino)

Putter. (1) A fragile instrument which sails beautifully when properly thrown. (Dan Jenkins) (2) There are two kinds. Hot and cold. (Joe James, in *Kill It Before It Moves,* 1961)

Rough. Playing area.

Rules. "Code ignored by your opponent." (Fred Beck, from *To Hell With Golf*)

Sand wedge. Special club used to blast one's ball out of sand traps, not to be confused with lunch. Chi Chi Rodriguez, talking of his accent, once noted, "It's still embarrassing. I asked my caddie for a sand wedge, and ten minutes later he came back with a ham on rye."

Score. A record of suffering much like a thermometer. The higher it goes, the greater the suffering. (*How to Give Up Golf* by Joe James, 1970)

Scorekeeper. Tee-totaler.

Scuffing/shanking. Trick shots in which the ball heads off in amazing directions. Used only to awe others.

Shelter. Small huts which you see in the distance when the rain comes on. (John D. Sheriden, in *It Stance to Reason*, 1947)

Short putt. Any putt you miss. (Grantland Rice and Clare Briggs, in *The Duffer's Handbook of Golf*)

Skill. Describing a great drive or long, difficult putt by one's self. Contrast with *act of God*, which describes a great drive or long, difficult putt by an opponent.

Slice. (1) The great soul crusher of all time. (Grantland Rice and Clare Briggs, in *The Duffer's Handbook of Golf*) (2) Probably most widely used golf swing. (Joe James, in *Kill It Before It Moves*, 1961)

Snowman. A score of 8.

-somes. Suffix for the number of golfers teeing off together. Hence a foursome is four players, a threesome is three golfers, a twosome is a pair, and a onesome is an individual with body odor. In *What It Is, Is Golf* (1965), author Joe James suggests that any group over a fivesome be known as a "gangsome" and any group that dallies on the greens and loses at least a ball a hole be known as a "gruesome."

Stance. One foot on floor, other on rail, right elbow on [clubhouse] bar, left hand holding out wallet. (author Dan Jenkins)

Subgolfer. Term created by Harry Leon Wilson in his 1923 work *So This Is Golf*: "The supergolfer has style and hence is called a stylist. The golfer has form, but is not hence called a formist. For some reason this word has not yet been invented. But the subgolfer has neither form nor style and is never called much of anything worth repeating. Yet let it be said at once that we are the only class of golfers of any real importance to the game. We are its spine and sinews, comprising ninety-two percent of its players. Lacking us the supergolfer could not play his tournaments nor be photographed for "Golf, Pastry and Plumbing."

Tee. A wooden tack on the head of which the ball sits while the player digs a moat around it. (Richard Sneddon, in *The Golf Stream*, 1941)

Tournament. A golfing fiesta, in preparation for which club members spend thousands of dollars for lessons and new equipment, in order to attempt winning a small cup worth about ten bucks. (Lawrence Larier, in *Golf and Be Damned*)

Trap. (1) Shallow hole which is filled with sand and angry golfers. Called a trap because many golfers act like wild animals when they get into one. (2) "What your opponent opens as you are about to make a shot." (Fred Beck, from *To Hell With Golf*)

Tree. Hostile, agile growth that jumps out of your opponent's way.

Water hazard. (1) Area of golf course designed to collect and wash golf balls, particularly brand-new ones. (Tom Carey, from *Teed Off*) (2) Large numbers of golf balls, covered with water to prevent recovery by anyone but the pro shop. (*How to Give Up Golf* by Joe James, 1970)

Woods. What most golfers can't keep out of. (Richard Sneddon, in *The Golf Stream*, 1941)

Yips. (1) Affliction that causes golfers faced with short putts to tremble, sweat, twitch, and miss. (2) Sounds opponent makes when golfer misses short putt. (Tom Carey, from *Teed Off*)

Afterwords

•**Hagemann's Law.** Those who have all the answers usually don't know what the questions are.

—John F. Hagemann

The *Official Rules for Golfers* is the fourth work in a series of books that attempts to describe elements of the real world through laws, rules, principles, and maxims. More are on the way, including one on travel and transportation, which will, among other things, attempt to solve the old question of why there is never a Gate 1 at the airport.

Needless to say, the Director is ever eager to collect new laws and hear from readers. Write to me at this address:

Paul Dickson
Director for Life
The Murphy Center & Golf Club
P.O. Box 80
Garrett Park, MD 20896-0080

In addition to new laws and maxims, the Director is particularly interested in anyone who can help with one tiny personal golfing flaw that, for lack of a more precise name, he calls his toe-ing-shanking-scuffing-topping-slicing-hooking flaw.

Particular thanks for help with this work go to Dave Kelly of the Library of Congress for helping me locate bits of sage golfing lore dating back into the last century, and to Bob Skole, who actually snagged one of the best laws in the book from a fellow passenger on a transatlantic flight. Also thanks to Bill Mead, Stephen B. Wells, and Jack Limpert for their help with the manuscript.

Index

111

Television. Mead's List
Temper. Lord Avebury's
  Summation on Golf and
  Life, Batchelor's Proverbs
Tension. O'Loughlin's
  Confession
**Theological Aspects of
  Golf.** Graham's
  Theological Exception, Tee
  Talk, Trevino's Theological
  Advice
**Thermodynamics of the
  Game.** Duffer's Laws
Time. Howson's Theorem,
  Jump's Discovery, Nixon's
  Trade-Off, Scott-Cousins
  Rules
Topping the Ball. Fables
  for Golfers, Revised
  Proverbs
Tourists. Cannon's Razor
Trade. Campbell's
  Economic Truism
Trees. Duffer's Laws,

Johnson's Percentage,
Metz's Rules of Golf for
Good Players, Revised
Proverbs

War, Golf as. Ike's Advice
  to Golfers
Water. Duffer's Laws
White Shoes. Cannon's
  Razor
Winds. Shakespeare the
  Golfer
Women's Golf. Lord
  Wellwood's Bid
Work, Golf and. Essex Golf
  Club Analogy, Hope's
  Distinction, Jones's
  Confession, Melville's
  Revision, Pillow Talk,
  Sneddon's Warning
Wrong Ball. Lemon's Law
  of the Links
Wrongheaded Advice.
  Don'ts for the Duffer